GIGANTIC (SAUROPOD) DINOSAURS

DINO-SORTED!

CLASSIFY THE FEATURES OF PREHISTORIC CREATURES

SONYA NEWLAND

Gareth Stevens PUBLISHING

Please visit our website, www.garethstevens.com. For a free color catalog of all our high-quality books, call toll free 1-800-542-2595 or fax 1-877-542-2596.

Cataloging-in-Publication Data
Names: Newland, Sonya.

Title: Gigantic dinosaurs / Sonya Newland.
Description: Buffalo, NY : Gareth Stevens Publishing, 2026. | Series: Dino-sorted! | Includes glossary and index.
Identifiers: ISBN 9781482473636 (pbk.) | ISBN 9781482473643 (library bound) | ISBN 9781482473650 (ebook)
Subjects: LCSH: Saurischia--Juvenile literature. | Saurischia--Classification--Juvenile literature.
Classification: LCC QE862.S3 N483 2026 | DDC 567.912--dc23

Published in 2026 by
Gareth Stevens Publishing
2544 Clinton St.
Buffalo, NY 14224

First published in Great Britain in 2021 by
The Watts Publishing Group

Credits
Editor: Sonya Newland
Designer: Clare Nicholas

The publisher would like to thank the following for permission to reproduce their pictures:

Alamy: Stocktrek Images, Inc. 6t, 9, 23t, The Natural History Museum 15b, 19, 22, Science Photo Library 21b; Shutterstock: SciePro 4l, Warpaint cover, §4r, 7t, 8–9, 11r, 27b, Catmando 5t, 15t, 16–17, 21t, 23b, Auntspray 5b, Kbel 6b, Herschel Hoffmeyer 7b, 18–19, 26, Zhenyakot 8b, Kostyantyn Ivanyshen 10, Josh Schneider 11t, olgasoi007 11bl, Teguh Mulyono 11br, Daniel Eskridge12–13, Dotted Yeti 13, Sakan.p 14t, Bob Orsillo 14b, William Cushman 17, Kostyantyn Ivanyshen 18, Linda Bucklin 20–21, 24–25, 28–29, 29, Kid Dog Travel 25, kamomeen 27t.

All design elements from Shutterstock.

Printed in the United States of America

CPSIA compliance information: Batch #CSGS26: For further information contact Gareth Stevens at 1-800-542-2595.

PRONUNCIATION GUIDE

Alamosaurus (ah-la-mow-SORE-us)

Amargasaurus (a-marg-oh-SORE-us)

Ampelosaurus (am-pel-oh-SORE-us)

Apatosaurus (ah-PAT-oh-SORE-us)

Argentinosaurus (AR-gent-ee-no-SORE-us)

Bajadasaurus (ba-had-ah-SORE-us)

Brachiosaurus (BRAK-ee-oh-SORE-us)

Camarasaurus (KAM-ar-a-SORE-us)

Cetiosauriscus (see-tee-oh-SORE-is-kus)

Cetiosaurus (see-TEE-oh-SORE-us)

Diplodocus (DIP-low-DOCK-us)

Mamenchisaurus (mah-men-chi-SORE-us)

Nigersaurus (nee-zhayr-SORE-us)

Patagotitan (pat-a-go-TIE-tun)

Saltasaurus (salt-a-SORE-us)

Shunosaurus (SHOON-oh-SORE-us)

Stegosaurus (steg-oh-SORE-us)

Supersaurus (SOO-per-SORE-us)

Titanosaurus (ty-TAN-oh-SORE-us)

Triceratops (try-SERRA-tops)

Tyrannosaurus rex (tie-RAN-oh-SORE-us recks)

CONTENTS

MEET THE

DINOSAURS CAN BE SORTED INTO GROUPS THAT SHARE CERTAIN FEATURES—AND THERE'S NO MISTAKING A SAUROPOD! WITH THEIR HUGE SIZE, THEIR BARREL-LIKE BODIES, AND THEIR LONG NECKS, THESE DINOSAURS ARE VERY DISTINCTIVE.

Apatosaurus

Cetiosaurus

About a quarter of all dinosaur species are sauropods. They belong to the saurischian, or "lizard-hipped," category of dinosaurs. All sauropods were herbivores that walked on four legs. They were the largest animals ever to roam Earth.

MID JURASSIC DINOSAURS

Cetiosaurus

LATE JURASSIC DINOSAURS

Apatosaurus
Brachiosaurus
Camarasaurus
Diplodocus
Mamenchisaurus
Shunosaurus
Supersaurus

EARLY CRETACEOUS DINOSAURS

Amargasaurus
Bajadasaurus

JURASSIC PERIOD
(201 to 145 million years ago)

SAUROPODS

Amargasaurus

Sauropods evolved in the Early Jurassic Period, 201–174 million years ago. They survived until the Late Cretaceous Period. Sauropod fossils have been found on every continent except Antarctica.

Around 66 million years ago, the sauropods were wiped out in a mass extinction event, along with the rest of the dinosaurs. Scientists believe that an asteroid crashed into Earth, filling the air with gas and dust. Earth's climate changed and it became too cold for the dinosaurs to survive.

MID CRETACEOUS DINOSAURS

Nigersaurus

LATE CRETACEOUS DINOSAURS

Alamosaurus
Ampelosaurus
Argentinosaurus
Patagotitan
Saltasaurus
Titanosaurus

CRETACEOUS PERIOD
(145 to 66 million years ago)

GIANT SIZE

SAUROPODS WERE THE GIANTS OF THE PREHISTORIC WORLD. EVEN THE SMALLER SPECIES OF SAUROPOD WERE MASSIVE COMPARED TO MOST ANIMALS TODAY.

The titanosaurs are a sub-group of sauropods. This family contains some of the most gigantic sauropod species. *Patagotitan*, *Argentinosaurus,* and *Supersaurus* could all grow to about 115 feet (35 m) from snout to tail tip. That's longer than a blue whale–the biggest creature alive today.

Paleontologists know about *Supersaurus*'s huge size from the discovery of a shoulder bone 7.8 feet (2.4 m) long!

Large, bulky bodies meant that the sauropods were also extremely heavy. This affected how they moved around. The heavier sauropods may have been able to reach speeds of only about 5 miles (8 km) per hour–no more than a quick walk for a human.

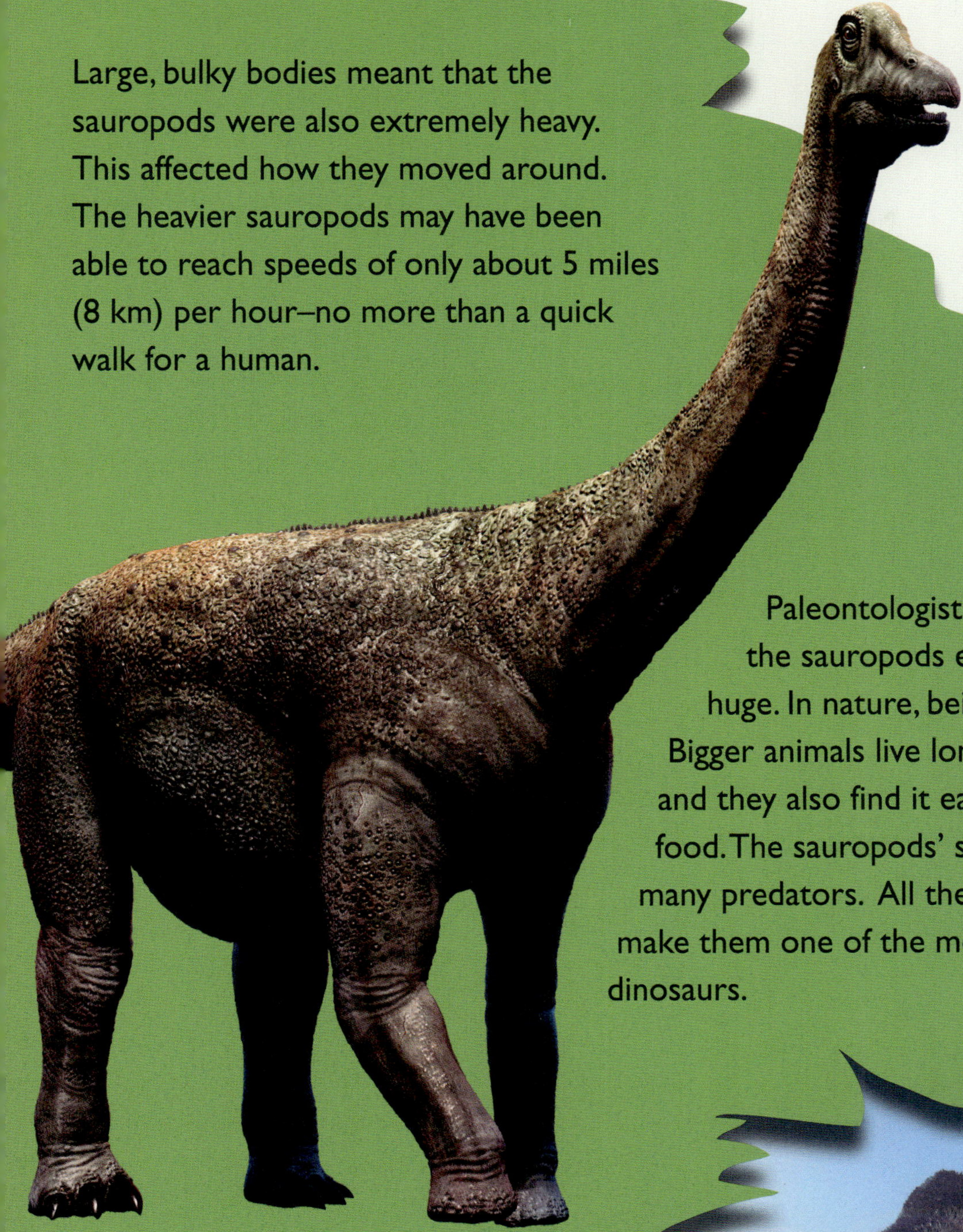

Smaller titanosaurs may have been able to move faster. *Saltasaurus* was about 40 feet (12 m) long–less than half the size of its largest relatives.

Paleontologists aren't certain why the sauropods evolved to become so huge. In nature, being big has advantages. Bigger animals live longer than small ones, and they also find it easier to compete for food. The sauropods' size would have put off many predators. All these factors helped to make them one of the most successful groups of dinosaurs.

Even large carnivores like *Tyrannosaurus rex* would struggle to kill a sauropod.

SORTED: ARGENTINOSAURUS

A GIANT EVEN AMONG THE TITANOSAURS, *ARGENTINOSAURUS* WAS ONE OF THE BIGGEST AND HEAVIEST CREATURES EVER TO HAVE EXISTED.

QUICK FACTS

PERIOD:
Late Cretaceous

LIVED IN:
South America

LENGTH:
Up to 115 feet (35 m)

WEIGHT:
155,000 pounds (70,000 kg)

HUGE BODY

It's hard to know for sure how big *Argentinosaurus* was because paleontologists have found bones from only some parts of its body. But fossils of its ribs, spine and leg bones suggest it was a huge animal. A single *Argentinosaurus* vertebra was as big as a human adult!

DINOMIGHTY!

Argentinosaurus is the heaviest known dinosaur. It weighed about as much as 12 African elephants.

GROWTH RATE

Argentinosaurus may have had a lifespan of more than 40 years. Experts estimate that it reached its full size at about the age of 23. It grew and put on weight very quickly. At one week old, a baby *Argentinosaurus* may have weighed twice as much as it did at birth! Humans take 2.5 years to double their birth weight.

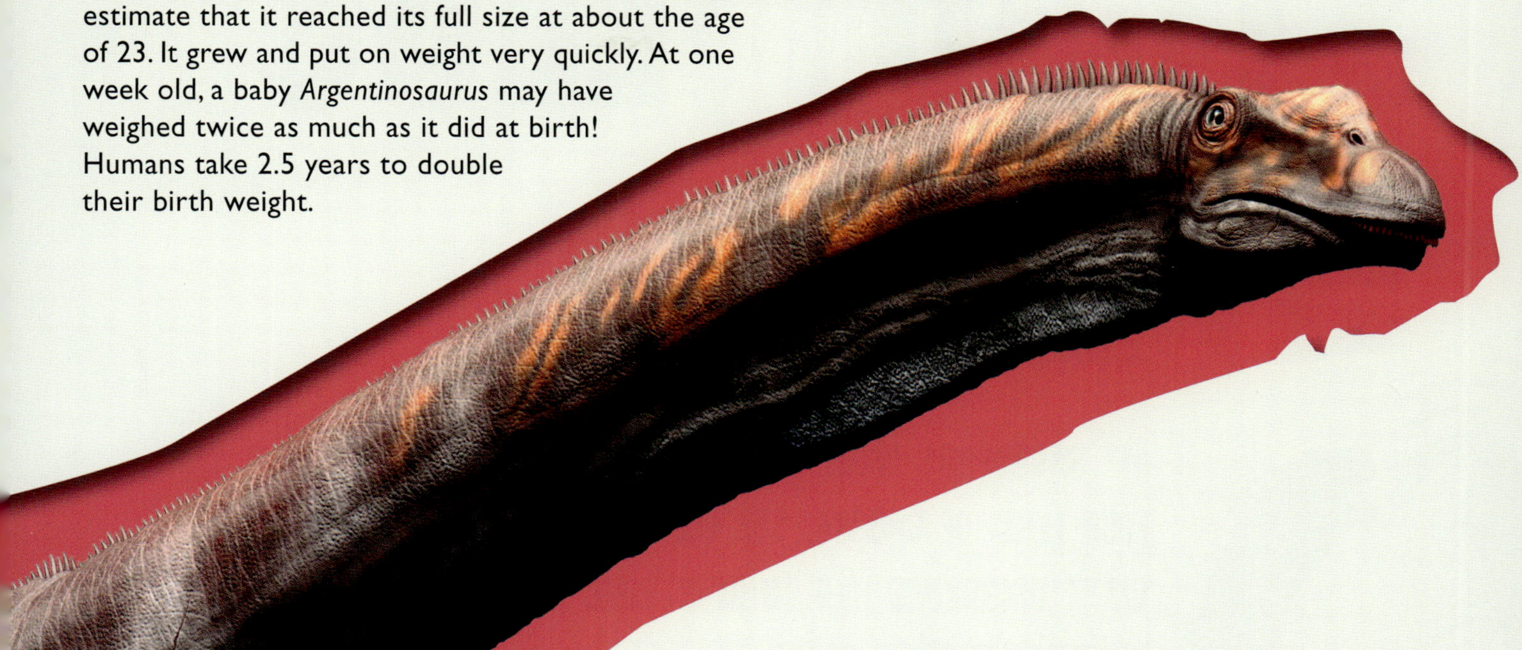

EGGS AND BABIES

Argentinosaurus eggs were probably about 1 foot (30 cm) long. Females may have laid up to 15 eggs at a time. The more eggs they laid, the better the chances one or more of the babies would survive. *Argentinosaurus* hatchlings weighed only around 11 pounds (5 kg), so hungry carnivores would have found it easy to prey on the baby sauropods.

STURDY LEGS AND FEET

ALL SAUROPODS WERE QUADRUPEDS. THEY WALKED ON FOUR LEGS. OF COURSE, THE LEGS AND FEET OF THESE GIANT DINOSAURS HAD TO BE STRONG AND STURDY TO SUPPORT THEIR HEAVY BODIES.

Sauropods had thick, powerful legs. Scientists describe them as "graviportal," which means they had evolved to bear their huge weight. In most sauropods, the back legs were longer and thicker than the front ones.

▲ Some sauropods may have been able to rear up on their hind legs, using their long tail for support. This would have helped them reach high leaves.

The sauropods had wide back feet, with five club-like toes. Each of the three inner toes had a large, flattened claw. Sauropods walked on the toes of their back feet, with the heel raised. A fleshy pad at the back of the foot supported the raised part.

Paleontologists have found sauropod footprints more than 3.3 feet (1 m) long. One print found in Australia measures 5.5 feet (1.7 m)!

In most heavy animals, the front feet spread outwards slightly to support more weight. The bones in a sauropod's front feet were arranged in an upright structure, like pillars. Some sauropods had a front "thumb claw," but others had no claws or even toes on their front feet.

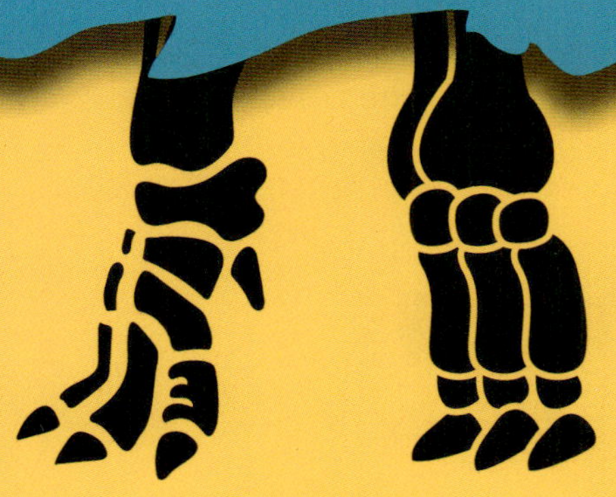

Elephant's front foot

Sauropod's front foot

Footprints from titanosaurs show that their feet were more like horseshoe-shaped stumps, with no toes.

SORTED:

BRACHIOSAURUS

BRACHIOSAURUS WAS AN UNUSUAL DINOSAUR. IT HAD LONG FRONT LEGS AND A VERY LONG NECK THAT IT HELD UP HIGH, LIKE A GIRAFFE.

HEAD

Brachiosaurus's skull was dome-shaped. It had a long, wide snout, which was good for stripping leaves from branches.

FRONT LEGS

Unlike most other sauropods, *Brachiosaurus*'s front legs were longer than its back ones. This is where *Brachiosaurus* gets its name, which means "arm lizard." The front legs may have evolved this way to give the dinosaur extra height to reach the lush leaves at the very top of the trees.

TOES AND CLAWS

Each of *Brachiosaurus*'s feet had five toes. There was a claw on the first toe of each front foot and on three toes of each back foot. The underside of each foot was protected by a pad of fleshy skin.

QUICK FACTS

PERIOD:
Late Jurassic

LIVED IN:
Africa, Europe, North America

LENGTH:
up to 98 feet (30 m)

WEIGHT:
125,000 pounds (56,000 kg)

DINOMIGHTY!

Brachiosaurus had to eat more than 440 pounds (200 kg) of plants every day–that's the weight of nearly 30 bowling balls.

WAY OF WALKING

Like other sauropods, *Brachiosaurus* bore its weight on the toes at the front of the feet. This gave it a "high-heeled" way of walking.

TEETH AND JAWS

COMPARED TO THEIR HUGE BODIES, SAUROPODS HAD VERY SMALL HEADS—AND VERY SMALL BRAINS! THEIR JAWS TOOK UP MOST OF THEIR SKULL.

The size, type, and number of teeth a sauropod had depended on its diet–delicate leaves from high up in the trees or tougher plants closer to the ground.

The joint of the jaw was positioned right at the back of the skull. A sauropod opened and closed its mouth in a kind of flip-top action. Sauropods had no cheeks, so it was difficult for them to chew. Instead, they stripped leaves off trees and bushes with their teeth and used their tongues to push this plant matter down their throats.

Some sauropods, such as *Camarasaurus* (see pages 24–25), had spoon-shaped teeth that gave them a strong bite. Others, such as *Diplodocus* (see pages 20–21) developed sharper, pencil-shaped teeth that were better for stripping leaves off branches.

The bigger sauropods may have had to eat about 100,000 calories a day. By comparison, humans need only about 2,000–2,500 calories to maintain their weight.

These pencil-shaped teeth are from *Cetiosauriscus*, the first sauropod to be discovered. *Cetiosauriscus* would have used these teeth to strip leaves from ferns and branches.

Sauropods ate almost constantly, so their teeth faced a lot of wear and tear. They would never last a lifetime. Instead, rows of teeth grew one behind the other so they could be continually replaced. Most sauropods had a completely new set of teeth every few weeks.

SORTED:

NIGERSAURUS

AT AROUND 50 FEET (15 M) LONG, *NIGERSAURUS* WAS SMALL FOR A SAUROPOD. IT WAS ALSO ONE OF THE STRANGEST-LOOKING MEMBERS OF THE SAUROPOD FAMILY!

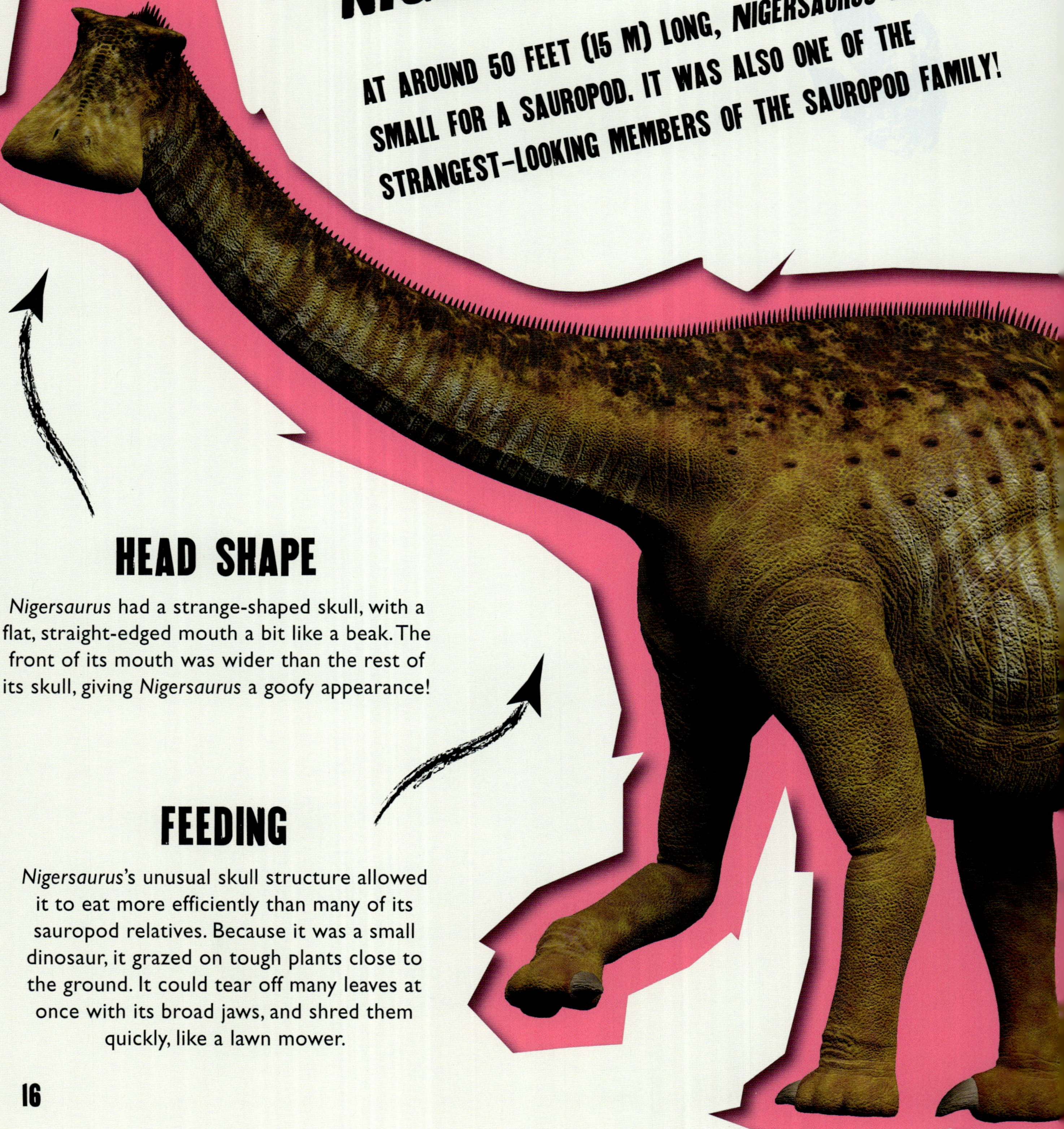

HEAD SHAPE

Nigersaurus had a strange-shaped skull, with a flat, straight-edged mouth a bit like a beak. The front of its mouth was wider than the rest of its skull, giving *Nigersaurus* a goofy appearance!

FEEDING

Nigersaurus's unusual skull structure allowed it to eat more efficiently than many of its sauropod relatives. Because it was a small dinosaur, it grazed on tough plants close to the ground. It could tear off many leaves at once with its broad jaws, and shred them quickly, like a lawn mower.

QUICK FACTS

PERIOD:
Mid Cretaceous

LIVED IN:
Africa

LENGTH:
up to 50 feet (15 m)

WEIGHT:
8,820 pounds(4,000 kg)

TEETH

In its odd jaw, *Nigersaurus* had hundreds of small, needle-shaped teeth, arranged in around 50 columns. Behind each tooth, up to nine others were lined up ready to replace it. Paleontologists think that all *Nigersaurus*'s teeth wore down and were replaced at the same time.

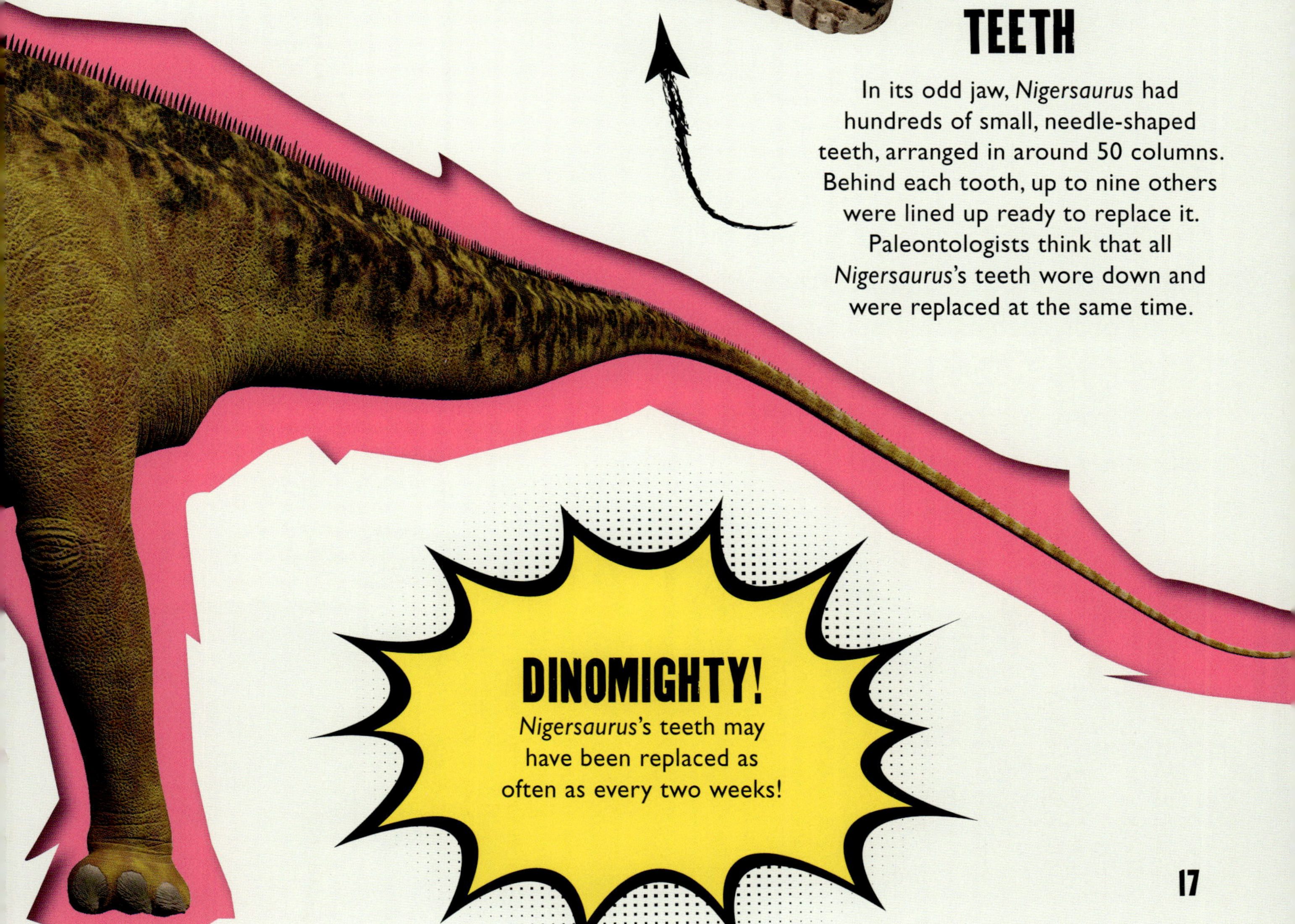

DINOMIGHTY!

Nigersaurus's teeth may have been replaced as often as every two weeks!

LONG NECK AND TAIL

SAUROPODS CAN BE EASILY IDENTIFIED BY THEIR LONG NECKS AND TAILS. BUT HOW AND WHY DID THIS GROUP OF DINOSAURS EVOLVE TO HAVE THESE ENORMOUS BODY PARTS?

The sauropods' long necks allowed them to pluck leaves from the tallest trees, where smaller herbivores, such as *Stegosaurus* or *Triceratops*, couldn't reach. They may also have swept their necks from side to side to help them graze efficiently near the ground.

Sauropods, such as *Mamenchisaurus*, used their long neck to eat from wide areas of land as they lumbered along.

No one knows for sure in what position sauropods held their necks. Some experts think they held them straight out in front. Others suggest that the neck was held upright, like an ostrich's. It may have been somewhere in between, and perhaps varied between different members of the sauropod family.

Paleontologists look at the vertebrae and shoulder bones of sauropod species like this *Shunosaurus* to try to work out how they held their necks.

Sauropods all had long, muscular tails that helped to balance the weight of their huge necks and bodies. The tails tapered at the end, like whips. These strong tails made effective weapons for lashing out at attackers.

Some experts think that larger sauropods might have been able to whip their tails faster than the speed of sound!

SORTED:

DIPLODOCUS

QUICK FACTS

PERIOD:
Late Jurassic

LIVED IN:
North America

LENGTH:
up to 85 feet (26 m)

WEIGHT:
44,000 pounds (20,000

***DIPLODOCUS* IS ONE OF THE BEST-KNOWN DINOSAURS THANKS TO ITS AMAZING LENGTH—AND ITS TINY BRAIN!**

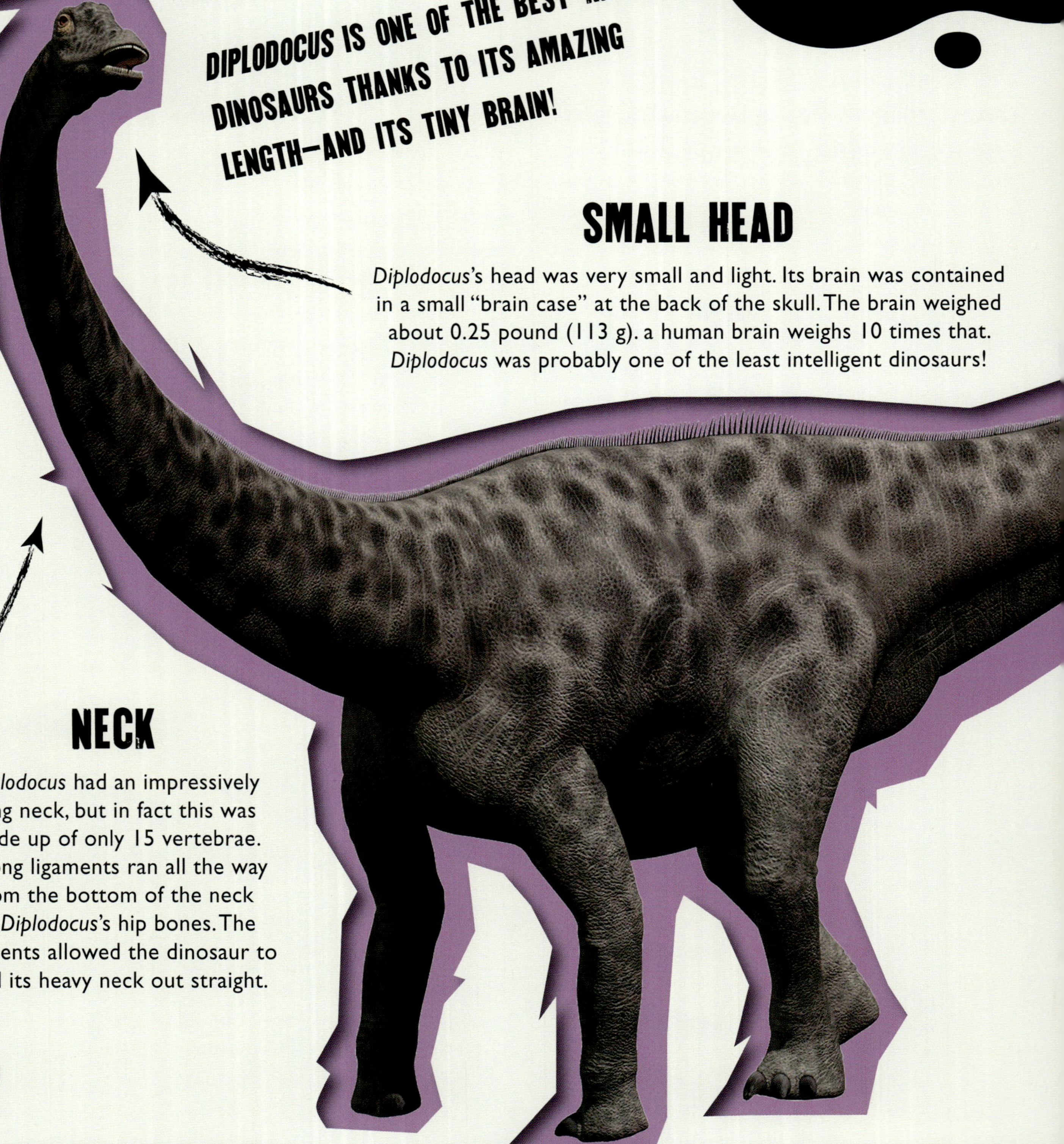

SMALL HEAD

Diplodocus's head was very small and light. Its brain was contained in a small "brain case" at the back of the skull. The brain weighed about 0.25 pound (113 g). a human brain weighs 10 times that. *Diplodocus* was probably one of the least intelligent dinosaurs!

NECK

Diplodocus had an impressively long neck, but in fact this was made up of only 15 vertebrae. Strong ligaments ran all the way from the bottom of the neck to *Diplodocus*'s hip bones. The ligaments allowed the dinosaur to hold its heavy neck out straight.

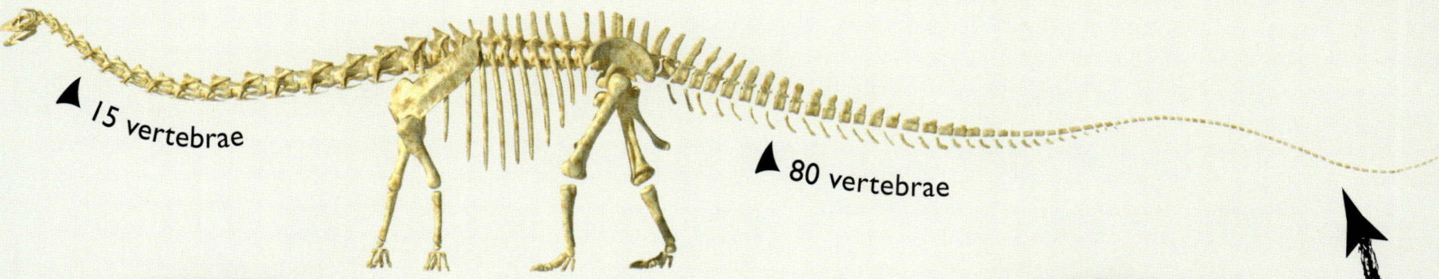

TAIL

Diplodocus's tail contained 80 bones, which made it very flexible. This long tail made up half the dinosaur's total length and weight, and helped balance its neck. *Diplodocus*'s back leg muscles anchored its tail, so it may have been able to rear up on its hind legs.

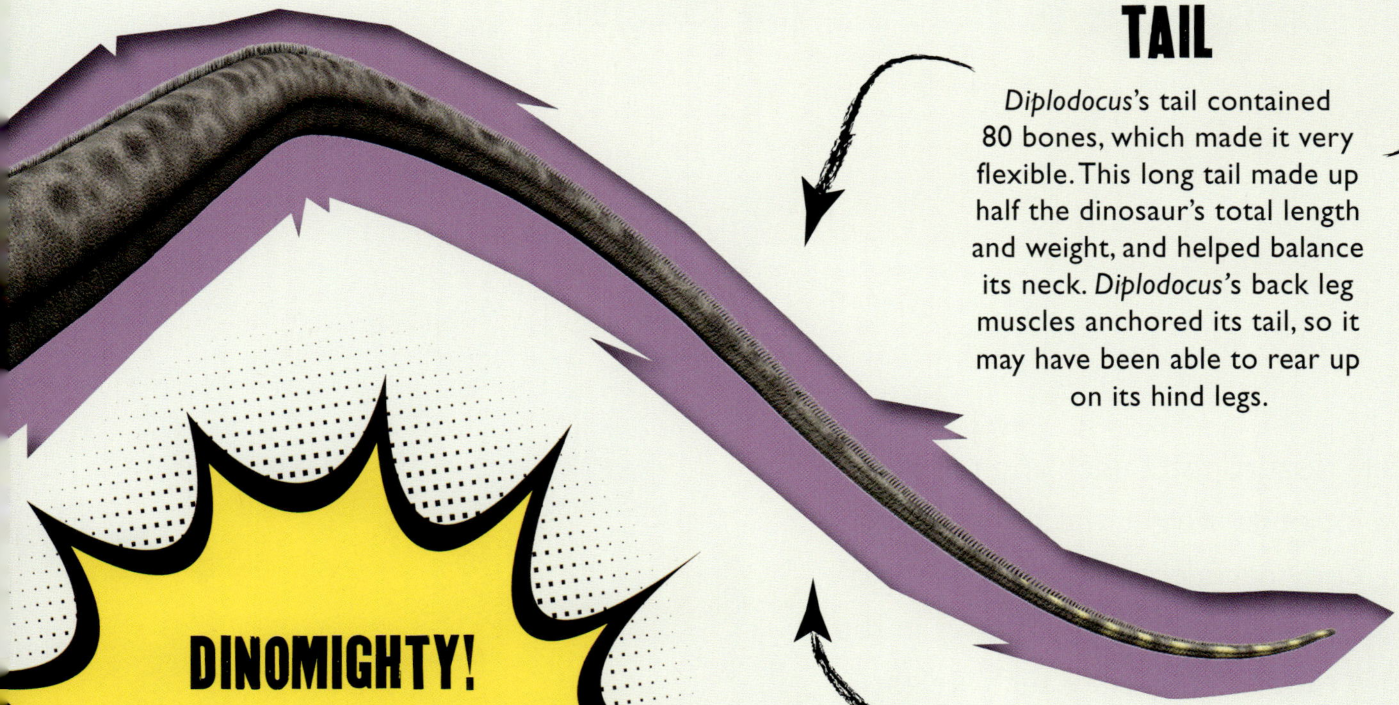

DINOMIGHTY!

The longest-necked animal in the world today is an adult male giraffe, whose neck can grow up to 7.8 feet (2.4 m) long. *Diplodocus*'s neck was three times that length!

DOUBLE BEAMS

On the underside of its tail, *Diplodocus* had two rows of bones attached to the vertebrae, which gave it important extra support. This is where it gets its name, which means "double beam."

BONES AND BLOOD

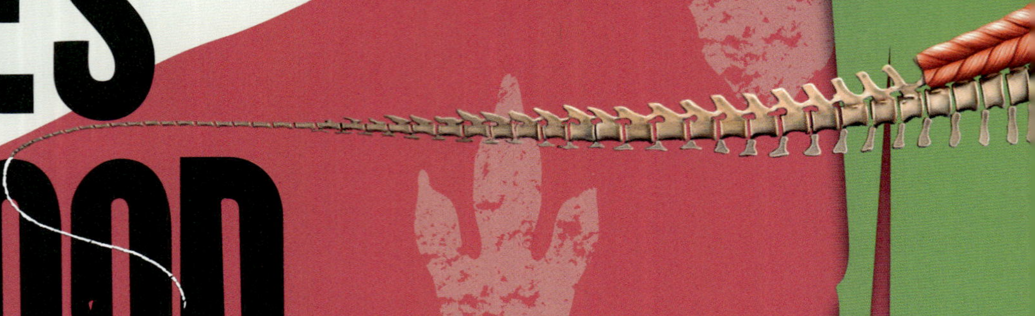

HOW DID SAUROPODS GROW SO HUGE WITHOUT BECOMING TOO HEAVY TO STAND OR MOVE? AND HOW DID AIR AND BLOOD TRAVEL AROUND THEIR BIG BODIES EFFICIENTLY ENOUGH TO KEEP THEM ALIVE? THE ANSWER LIES IN THE SAUROPODS' BONE STRUCTURE.

While a sauropod's neck and tail made up a lot of its weight, the bones in these long body parts contained hundreds of air sacs. These holes and hollows in the bones reduced the dinosaur's weight while maintaining its strength.

➤ Air pockets in the vertebrae stopped the neck from being so heavy that the sauropod would not be able to lift it.

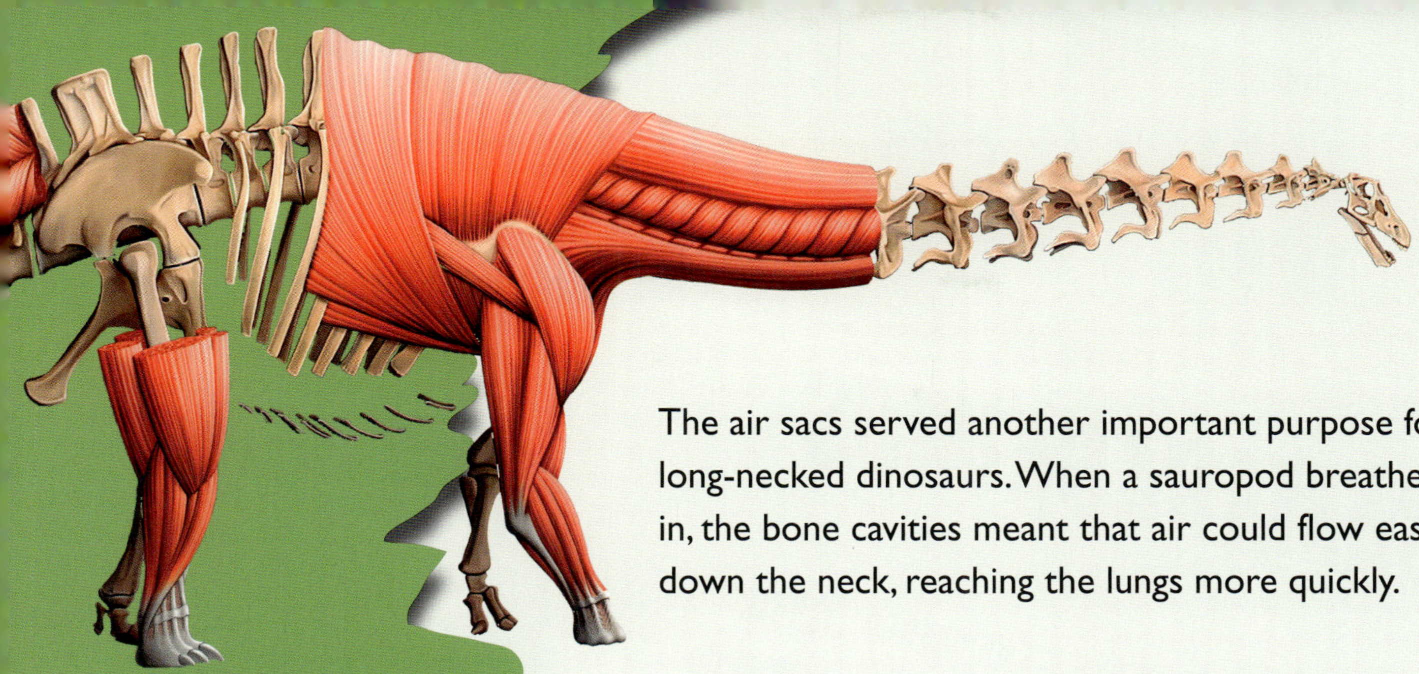

The air sacs served another important purpose for long-necked dinosaurs. When a sauropod breathed in, the bone cavities meant that air could flow easily down the neck, reaching the lungs more quickly.

The hollow vertebrae in the neck, back, and tail were supported by other light bones. Sauropods also had strong muscles in their neck, their legs, and the top of their tail.

One of the biggest mysteries about the sauropods is how they pumped enough blood up their long necks to reach their brains. Paleontologists once thought that they may have had two hearts! They don't think that any more, but sauropod hearts must have been very big to pump blood all around their vast bodies.

The way blood flowed around a sauropod's body must have been designed to stop a huge rush of blood to the head whenever the dinosaur lowered its neck.

SORTED:

CAMARASAURUS

CAMARASAURUS MEANS "CHAMBERED LIZARD." PALEONTOLOGISTS NAMED THIS SMALL SAUROPOD AFTER THE "CHAMBERS," OR HOLLOWS, THEY NOTICED IN ITS BONES WHEN THEY DISCOVERED IT.

QUICK FACTS

PERIOD:
Late Jurassic

LIVED IN:
North America

LENGTH:
up to 50 feet (18 m)

WEIGHT:
44,000 pounds (20,000 kg)

VERTEBRAE

When *Camarasaurus* was first discovered in 1877, people thought the hollows in its vertebrae simply reduced its weight. Now, experts believe they were also part of its respiratory system. The channels in the bones carried vital oxygen to the lungs.

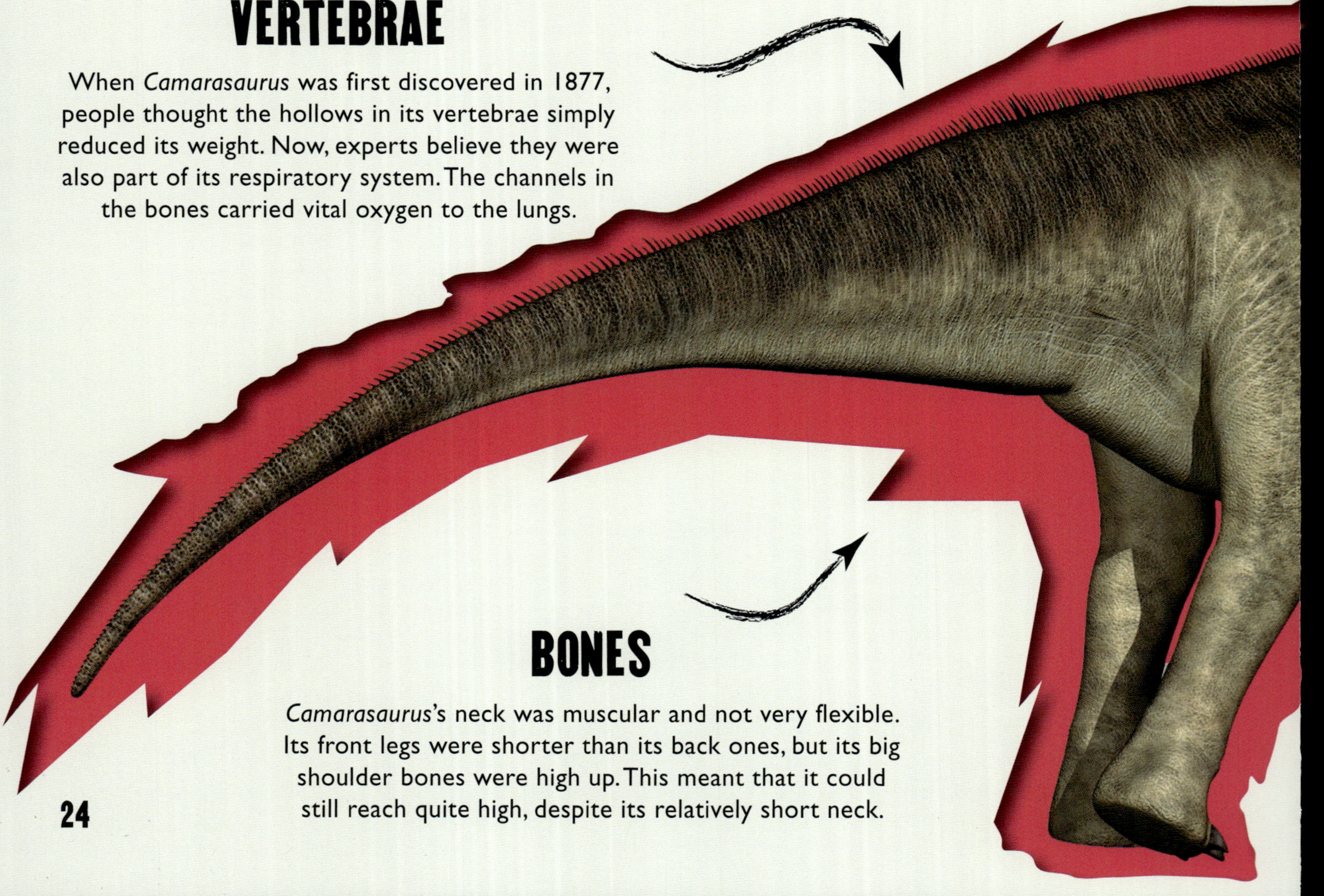

BONES

Camarasaurus's neck was muscular and not very flexible. Its front legs were shorter than its back ones, but its big shoulder bones were high up. This meant that it could still reach quite high, despite its relatively short neck.

DINOMIGHTY!

Camarasaurus was one of the most successful dinosaurs. Many fossils of this sauropod have been discovered, including some complete ones. This suggests that there were a lot of them around!

TWO BRAINS?

In *Camarasaurus* and other sauropod fossils, part of the backbone near the hips is enlarged. Scientists once thought this might have housed a second brain. In fact, it was probably a type of energy store called a glycogen body. Modern birds have this feature.

ARMOR AND WEAPONS

THE SAUROPODS WERE SO BIG THAT NOT MANY PREDATORS WOULD TRY TO ATTACK THEM. HOWEVER, SOME SAUROPOD FOSSILS SHOW EVIDENCE OF INJURIES, WHICH SUGGESTS THAT THEIR SIZE DIDN'T ALWAYS KEEP THEM SAFE.

Sauropods all had thick, leathery skin that would have been tough to bite through. For extra protection, some sauropods–including the titanosaurs–developed bony lumps called osteoderms on their back and sides. These were embedded in the skin rather than being part of the skeleton.

Saltasaurus was one of the first known sauropods to have the bony body armor called osteoderms.

A few sauropods had rows of spines on their necks, backs or tails. These would have made it painful for any predator who tried to take a bite out of them. A recently discovered dinosaur called *Bajadasaurus* may have had a row of very long spines along its neck– a warning to any carnivore on the attack!

Amargasaurus had double rows of tall, sharp spikes on its head and neck, and running the length of its back and tail.

A sauropod's tail could be a useful weapon. The tail was made up of lots of vertebrae, which made it very flexible. They were also strong and heavy. A sauropod could lash its tail with lightning speed, injuring or even killing an attacker.

Shunosaurus had a small club at the end of its tail that could do predators serious damage!

SORTED:

AMPELOSAURUS

QUICK FACTS

PERIOD:
Late Cretaceous

LIVED IN:
Europe

LENGTH:
50 feet (15 m)

WEIGHT:
up to 22,000 pounds (10,000 kg)

***AMPELOSAURUS* BELONGS TO A GROUP OF TITANOSAURS CALLED LITHOSTROTIA, WHICH MEANS "PAVED WITH STONES." IT'S A SUITABLE NAME FOR THIS ARMORED DINOSAUR!**

PLATES AND SPIKES

Ampelosaurus was small compared to many other sauropods. This might have made it a target for attack if it hadn't been for its well-protected body. Thick, bony plates covered its back. On top of these were many knobby spikes.

ARMOR ARRANGEMENT

Paleontologists think the osteoderms on titanosaurs like *Ampelosaurus* were arranged in two rows, side by side. This is similar to the way the plates were arranged on the back of the stegosaurs, the best-known "armored dinosaurs."

OSTEODERMS

Like other titanosaurs, *Ampelosaurus*'s osteoderms (see pages 26–27) were fixed in its skin. They came in three different shapes: plates, bulbs, and spines. Plates were thick pieces of bone that lay flat against the skin. Bulbs were small lumps. The spines were the pointiest parts of the bony armor.

DINOMIGHTY!

More than 500 *Ampelosaurus* bones have been found, which means that experts know quite a lot about this Late Cretaceous sauropod.

GLOSSARY

AIR SACS – holes in bones that reduce their weight

ASTEROID – a large rock that forms in space and orbits the sun

CARNIVORE – an animal that eats meat

CONTINENT – one of the seven large landmasses on Earth

EVOLVE – to change and develop gradually over time

FOSSIL – the shape of a plant or animal that has been preserved in rock for a very long time

HATCHLING – a baby animal just after it has hatched from an egg

HERBIVORE – an animal that eats only plants and fruit

LIGAMENT – strong, stringy tissue that connects bones in the body

MASS EXTINCTION – the death of many living things

OSTEODERMS – small lumps of bone in the skin of an animal

OXYGEN – a gas in the air that animals need to breathe

PALEONTOLOGIST – a scientist who studies dinosaurs and prehistoric life

PREDATOR – an animal that hunts and kills other animals for food

QUADRUPED – describing an animal that walks on four legs rather than two

RESPIRATORY SYSTEM – the body system related to breathing and carrying oxygen into and around the body

RIBS – the long, thin bones in the chest that protect the heart and lungs

SAURISCHIAN – one of the two main categories of dinosaurs, called "lizard-hipped" because they all had a pelvis similar to that of modern reptiles

SKULL – the bones that make up the head and face

SPECIES – a group of living things that are closely related and share similar features

SUB-GROUP – a group of animals within a larger category that have particular features in common

VERTEBRAE – the bones that make up the spine, or backbone (singular: vertebra)

FURTHER INFORMATION

BOOKS

Why? Dinosaurs
By Stephanie Warren Drimmer (National Geographic Kids, 2025)

Diplodocus
By Nicki Calusen-Grace (Black Rabbit Books, 2025)

ACTIVITY

Use the information in this book to design a new sauropod species. Remember to include all the features of sauropods. Then give your dinosaur a name.

WEBSITES

www.amnh.org/explore/news-blogs/news-posts/know-your-sauropod
Get to know the sauropods with this article from the American Museum of Natural History.

https://kids.nationalgeographic.com/animals/prehistoric
Learn more about all kinds of dinosaurs here.

INDEX